In 2007 Sarah Hanson-Young became the youngest woman ever to be elected to the Australian parliament. With over a decade in politics as a Greens Senator, Sarah is a leading voice for progressive change. She lives in the Adelaide Hills with her optimistic eleven-year-old daughter, Kora.

Writers in the *On Series*

Fleur Anderson
Gay Bilson
John Birmingham
Julian Burnside
Blanche d'Alpuget
Paul Daley
Robert Dessaix
Juliana Engberg
Sarah Ferguson
Nikki Gemmell
Stan Grant
Germaine Greer
Sarah Hanson-Young
Jonathan Holmes
Daisy Jeffrey
Susan Johnson
Malcolm Knox

Barrie Kosky
Sally McManus
David Malouf
Paula Matthewson
Katharine Murphy
Dorothy Porter
Leigh Sales
Mark Scott
Tory Shepherd
Tim Soutphommasane
David Speers
Natasha Stott Despoja
Anne Summers
Tony Wheeler
Ashleigh Wilson
Elisabeth Wynhausen

Sarah Hanson-Young

En Garde

hachette
AUSTRALIA

Every attempt has been made to locate the copyright holders for material quoted in this book. Any person or organisation that may have been overlooked or misattributed may contact the publisher.

Published in Australia and New Zealand in 2020
by Hachette Australia
(an imprint of Hachette Australia Pty Limited)
Level 17, 207 Kent Street, Sydney NSW 2000
www.hachette.com.au

First published in 2018 by Melbourne University Publishing

10 9 8 7 6 5 4 3 2 1

Copyright © Sarah Hanson-Young 2018

This book is copyright. Apart from any fair dealing for the purposes of private study, research, criticism or review permitted under the *Copyright Act 1968*, no part may be stored or reproduced by any process without prior written permission. Enquiries should be made to the publisher.

 A catalogue record for this book is available from the National Library of Australia

ISBN: 978 0 7336 4446 7 (paperback)

Original cover concept by Nada Backovic Design
Author photograph by Andrew Correll
Text design by Alice Graphics
Typeset by Typeskill
Printed and bound in Australia by McPherson's Printing Group

 The paper this book is printed on is certified against the Forest Stewardship Council® Standards. McPherson's Printing Group holds FSC® chain of custody certification SA-COC-005379. FSC® promotes environmentally responsible, socially beneficial and economically viable management of the world's forests.

En garde

To be truthful, you must be vulnerable, and to be resilient, you must be aware of your own vulnerabilities.

For years, I let slide the sexist slurs and innuendo spoken against me, both inside and outside parliament, thinking that staying quiet and not making a fuss would eventually make it stop. I had convinced myself that not giving it oxygen would force it to fade away. I was wrong. As a woman who has a reputation for not being shy about standing up and calling things out, this silence led to a festering conflict inside me.

The insults got louder and the men hurling them grew bolder. It seemed their aim was to break me, to bully me out of doing my job. They never did shut me up—not fully, anyway—but there were plenty of times they came close.

Then I started to call this sort of behaviour out and, ever since, I've been wondering whether I'm resilient enough to handle the consequences. Being honest means being truthful about how vulnerable I am to their attacks. Am I up for the critics saying that I'm playing the victim, that I'm being precious, that I'm nothing more than an attention seeker, a snowflake or princess? I have to be up for this.

Thankfully, there are women, and men, across the country who've responded to the attacks, and to me calling them out, with support and care, undeterred by the lazy labels from critics, naysayers and trolls. Women and girls have been telling me their stories—horrible examples of sexism and abuse, and many of them far worse than I've experienced. For these women, my ability to speak out is important. There is strength in expressing vulnerability. My vulnerability empowers them and, in return, their belief empowers me.

Politics is, by its nature, a tough gig and therefore not for the faint-hearted. The increasingly rigorous debate about 'values' means things in and around parliament often become intensely passionate and personal. I've always given as good as I get—debating issues and pushing for the ideas I believe in. I've never been too shy to say I agree or disagree with something. So, I'm used to the rough and tumble, but that doesn't mean I like it or that it's easy. While I'm talking about what we can do to make this country better, I'm constantly preparing for the insults to start flying. I'm in the parliament to debate policies, not to be attacked for my sex life or because I'm a mother. Sadly, despite many people saying they play the ball and not the man, or the woman, the opposite is often true.

Until recently, I thought being resilient meant not admitting that I was being bullied. I thought that doing so would show I was weak, but I was mistaken. It turns out that real strength comes from admitting to and confronting being bullied. It's hard, much harder than ignoring it, but it's the only way to make change.

I am aware that my ability to appear resilient in the face of attacks, or to weather the embarrassment that comes from my mistakes, can make me seem indomitable. People describe me as 'cold' and 'defensive' just as ambitious women are described as 'fierce' and 'nasty'. Whether the allegations are true or not, their narrative prevails.

My guard has always been up because it's needed to be; I am always wondering where the next attack will come from.

Critics have accused me of being 'a nasty piece of work', while, in the next breath, saying I am a 'bleeding heart'. I've been accused of being a 'social justice warrior' and 'playing the victim' at the same time. These negative terms are used to belittle the ability of women with or without public profiles to speak honestly and compassionately, with strength and power.

I've found it hard to reconcile the fact that that I am both resilient and vulnerable. But I am, and that's okay.

My vulnerability allows me to be resilient, because, ultimately, it is to do with being true to myself and what I stand for. I think most people are the same.

Politicians should be real people, who feel things deeply. We should be motivated to make the world a better place, and be disgusted when we see injustice and inequality.

So, I am real, I am tough, but I am also vulnerable, and I won't apologise for it anymore. I've spent all that time with my guard up, only to realise that I'm more powerful when it's down. My opponents should consider this a warning.

En garde!

Little companion

My daughter's name, 'Kora', comes from the language of the Wonnarua Nation, the traditional land owners of the Hunter Valley in New South Wales. It means 'companion'. This is fitting because, from before she was born, she has been with me as I've navigated my way through the world of politics. We've grown up together, her as a kid and me as a politician. Together a family, neither of us knows a life without the juggling involved in politics and the curveballs that come with it.

Back in 2006, the same week I found out I'd won preselection for the Greens in the upcoming South Australian Senate race, I found out I was pregnant. I was in shock, mostly because doctors had told me that, despite falling pregnant and having an abortion when I was at university, I was unlikely to conceive naturally, as I'd developed polycystic ovary syndrome (PCOS). PCOS, despite its name, is a hormone disorder. Some women who have it suffer from cysts on their ovaries, but not all of them do. Other women experience symptoms of depression, weight gain, and excessive hair growth or loss. Despite the condition affecting up to 20 per cent of the female population, there is little public awareness of the disorder and many women don't even know they have it. Sadly, medical conditions like PCOS that relate to women's reproductive systems don't get the funding, research or public attention that they need.

Whether it's ovarian or cervical cancer, endometriosis or PCOS, it seems that things to do with a vagina are still too icky to talk about, let alone to raise the interest of health ministers so that they secure proper funding to tackle them. My symptoms were less severe than those of many other sufferers, but doctors had told me that when the time came that I wanted a baby, it would be nearly impossible for me to become pregnant without hormone treatment. Having had an abortion when I was nineteen gave this advice an extra sting.

With all of this in mind, the last thing I had expected after winning the top spot on the Greens Senate ticket was to discover that I was now also winning at conception.

So, there I was, twenty-four years old, preselected and pregnant. At that stage, the

Greens had never won a South Australian seat in the federal parliament. But Bob Brown was the leader of the party and Prime Minister John Howard was on the nose. He had refused to say sorry to the stolen generations or to sign the Kyoto Protocol. I could feel that the support for the Greens was about to increase. It didn't take me long to work out that I'd been given two very big opportunities and I would be crazy not to take them. The baby was due in April 2007 and the election was due by the end of that year.

Perhaps it was naivety or the excitement of the campaign, or both, but not once did I think that trying to pull off being a new mum while starting my political career was unreasonable. I knew it wouldn't be easy, of course, but I've always worked hard. Silver platters weren't handed out in my family; I was taught from a young age that if you wanted something, you go get it yourself. I never thought for a moment that anyone would complain about it or try to stop me. Working mums are everywhere, and many are far less supported and not in positions as flexible as mine. It wasn't the 1950s anymore, even though we did have Howard as PM. I had won the preselection fair and square, so what was the problem with me having a baby?

Plenty, apparently. From the moment I started telling people inside the party that I was expecting, the grumbles started. 'You really should have told people you wanted to have a baby before you contested the preselection,' one male party member said to me. It wasn't the reaction I had banked on. My joy at being an expectant mother quickly turned to disappointment when a group inside one of the local branches tried to have my preselection ruled invalid on the basis that I was now pregnant. They argued that members had not been given all the relevant information before voting in the ballot. While it was never actually said, the meaning was clear: they were accusing me of concealing wanting a child, when, all the while, I had thought it was impossible. Why on earth would I reveal to a group of party members that I had skipped a period, or that I had a medical disorder that affected my fertility? These are questions a male candidate would never have been asked nor was it information he would ever be expected to divulge.

Thankfully, reason prevailed and the campaign against me was quietly dropped. Even so while the complaints were never formalised, they hung around in the background as mutterings and the odd snide comment, like unsubstantiated gripes often do, acting as a reminder that people were watching me and that some, perhaps, were waiting for me to fail.

One person's comments, when Bob Brown was in Adelaide to announce my candidature to the media, I will never forget. The press were keen on the story because the Greens' vote was growing, while the Democrats' had crashed, and I was a young woman stepping into politics at the same time former Democrats senator Natasha Stott Despoja was bowing out. The headline in *The Australian* the next day called me 'the Green Natasha', as though my age and gender were all that mattered.

Ten minutes before the press conference was due to start, a senior woman from the party came over to tell me exactly what she thought. 'So, you're having a baby?' she asked. 'Yes,' I said, on some level still expecting, from a colleague, the customary positive response to news of a pregnancy. 'That's a mistake,' she said, implying I was guaranteed to fail. She also said I should forget about trying to keep a partner because 'that would soon be over'.

I was floored.

Who says that? And, especially, who says that to another woman? A younger, female colleague who was looking for support? I was twenty weeks' pregnant and about to front the waiting media to announce the start of my political career. I bit my tongue, smiled and told her I hoped she was wrong. I felt small and I felt ill, though that could also have been morning sickness, which I was suffering from terribly at the time, but I knew from that moment I had to work harder than ever to pull this off. I had to make sure she was wrong. As motivation, there's nothing quite like proving those who doubt you wrong. I walked out to where the media were assembled and found Bob Brown waiting for me. He looked at me and said, with a big, warm smile, 'Babies are wonderful, just wonderful. This is great news!'

Kora was born in February, seven weeks early. She was perfectly healthy, but such a tiny little thing. I hit the campaign trail almost immediately, with bub, nappy bag and optimism all in tow. By the end of November,

I had been elected, and was not just the first Green from South Australia, but the youngest woman ever to be elected to any Australian parliament.

I was off to Canberra, with my little companion by my side.

Calling it out

I can't tell the story of how I decided to stand up to the bullying and sexism that has infected the Australian parliament without explaining what happened with Senator David Leyonhjelm on the chamber floor earlier this year.

That said, just as the straw alone didn't break the camel's back, this one incident doesn't explain the range of issues facing women in today's society, or why I've decided to call out the problems we in Australian politics face. Sexism in our media and public life has a long and torrid history that can't be encapsulated in one exchange. This is simply one part of my story—it just happens also to be the moment that I decided I'd had enough.

It started in June 2018, when former One Nation senator Fraser Anning asked the Senate to vote on whether the best thing to do to prevent the assault, rape and murder of women would be to arm them.

This is just one of a series of tired old arguments used to make women feel responsible for the violence that they are so regularly subjected to in Australia. It came off the back of the rape and murder in Melbourne of Eurydice Dixon, a comedian, who was found dead in a park only blocks from her home. This horrifying incident had sent ripples across the Australian community and people were angry; how could a young woman be so unsafe in her own city, simply because of daring to walk home from work at night? Vigils were held across the country, including at Parliament House in Canberra.

Senator Anning's motion called for the law to be changed to allow the 'importation of pepper spray, mace and tasers for individual self-defence', and called on state governments to legalise and actively promote the carrying of the weapons for women's 'personal protection'. It was a nasty, ham-fisted attempt at exploiting public concern regarding violence against women to bolster a dangerous campaign, championed by a number of right-wing MPs, to weaken gun control and the regulation of weapon imports.

Putting the responsibility on women to defend themselves is the same cheap trick as asking, 'Why didn't she just fight back?' Or, 'Why did she choose to put herself in a dangerous situation?'

The truth is, every woman I know has felt unsafe or intimidated at some point, whether it was at a bar, walking home at night, in her workplace or, tragically, even in her own home. Maintaining the safety of women shouldn't require us to carry a weapon just in case someone wants to attack us.

I voted against the motion because I don't believe that putting more weapons on the streets will make women safer in their homes or in public. I fear that the opposite would be true. More weapons in circulation is dangerous for everyone, but especially so for women. I also don't think that women should continue to have to take responsibility for the violent crimes and behaviour that some men carry out against them.

I wasn't the only one who felt this motion was a bad idea. The majority of the Senate voted against it, including all Liberal, Labor and Greens members.

Liberal Democrat David Leyonhjelm, who voted in favour of the motion, found himself with few friends on his side of the chamber. Only five senators voted in favour. Not one woman was among them.

It was then that Leyonhjelm decided to attack me.

'You should stop shagging men, Sarah!' he yelled at me across the chamber.

I heard the words as clear as a bell. They flew across the chamber like bullets and jolted me, which is, of course, what they were designed to do. It wasn't the first time that comments about my sexuality or gender had been used to put me down, shut me up and unsettle me. I'd copped slurs like this before. And despite ignoring them, hoping they would stop, they'd got worse and got louder. As I sat on the red benches of the Senate, surrounded by my colleagues, who were seemingly unaware of the impact the interjection had just had on me, I realised I'd been naive. This was never going to end, not until I stopped pretending that it wasn't happening.

After the vote was complete, I walked over to Senator Leyonhjelm and asked if I'd heard him correctly.

'What did you just say to me?' I asked.

'I asked if you were off men yet,' he replied.

Stunned, I said, 'No, that's not what you said.'

'Well, if you know what I said, quote it back to me,' he smirked.

'You said "stop shagging men".'

'Yes, I did,' he replied.

Shocked by his brazen response, I told him, 'You're a creep.'

'Fuck off,' he snapped.

Shaken, I walked away. For the first time in my workplace, I had stood up for myself and drawn a line in the sand. For years, I'd winced and tried not to flinch at innuendos from male colleagues about my dress, my body and my supposed sex life. What started as mutterings while I was on my feet, speaking, or during a debate, over the years slowly became slurs shouted across the chamber floor.

I'd spent years steeling myself against abuse. I'd learned to not react at all when some members of parliament would taunt me with the names of men they implied I'd had sex with. These insults and accusations were used in an attempt to bully, intimidate and stop me from doing my job; weaponised words and rumours were regularly used to throw me off my game.

Given I had, for the first time, acknowledged the smears and received Senator Leyonhjelm's disturbing response, I knew I had to do something about it. I told the leader of the Greens, Richard Di Natale, what had happened. Shocked, he agreed to speak both to Leyonhjelm and the president of the Senate,

Scott Ryan. Despite both Senator Di Natale and President Ryan asking him to apologise privately, Leyonhjelm refused. I would hope, in any other workplace, if someone had been confronted by their workmates over behaviour like this, they would, as a reasonable person, engage in some self-reflection, admit their actions were uncalled for and say sorry. But not here, and definitely not him.

I knew then that I had no other choice but to break my silence and put what had occurred on the record. Otherwise, he would forever know that, despite his abuse upsetting me, I hadn't called him out, and, worst of all, hadn't stood up for myself. If I wanted the abuse to stop, I had to stop it now.

Enough was enough. As I scribbled down notes, to clarify what I would say when I got to my feet, I felt sick—that kind of sick where your stomach feels nauseated and empty at the same time. I knew that by saying something on the record, I would have to break my silence on the smears and sexualised bullying I had endured for years. It wasn't enough to say what had just happened and that would be it, case closed. Women who stand up and call out bullying, sexual assault or harassment always cop a backlash in return.

I knew some people would accuse me of being weak, of 'playing the victim' or the 'gender card'. Women are always disadvantaged when naming bad behaviour, particularly in an environment where 'rough and tumble' and robust debate are par for the course. I knew that me outing these comments would be used to attack me with more insults, rumour and innuendo. This is the consequence for so many women when they speak out. Be silent or be shamed, that's the choice. Not being silent invites questions about truth, character and whether the woman in question really is just a slut.

But I'd had enough of being silent.

I stood up, sought the call of the Senate president and started speaking. I called on Senator Leyonhjelm to withdraw his comments and asked him for an apology. Again, he refused.

In other workplaces, telling a woman to 'stop shagging men' and refusing to apologise for it would probably get you fired. In parliament, though, it landed Senator Leyonhjelm an interview on Sky News, which he used to double down on his abuse.

'Sarah is known for liking men,' he said. 'The rumours about her in parliament are well known.' He spent days going from one media outlet to another, making disgraceful comments like this and dragging my name through the mud at every opportunity.

Just when I thought it couldn't get any worse, I heard that Leyonhjelm had been on the radio station 3AW and gone even further, naming somebody on air who he, incorrectly, told listeners I'd had sex with.

Again, I had known this was coming; that I would be punished for standing up for myself.

And I was hurt and distressed. This bloke was out telling anyone who would listen to rumours he'd heard, or made up, about my sex life, insinuating they were relevant to how I do my job. Media organisations were lining up around the block to give him a platform to repeat his smears.

Leyonhjelm's assault continued. His suggestions that I am sexually promiscuous were offensive, but his excuses for the attacks on me were worse. He argued that I had 'provoked' him—a classic tactic bullies use to justify their behaviour—'she made me do it' or 'she asked for it'. Pathetic excuse, of course. He claimed that I had said 'all men were rapists'. It was a lie. I have never said those words, which anyone can see if they check Hansard, and of course I never would have because they're not true. He accused me of being a 'hypocrite' for both having sex with men and being concerned about violence some men commit against women.

He tried to excuse his behaviour by arguing his abuse had nothing to do with me being a woman. On ABC Radio National's breakfast program, Leyonhjelm defended his comments by saying, 'I think you're mischaracterising it as sexist abuse, when it's just abuse,' which, grotesquely, he described as being 'normal Australian behaviour'. For far too many women in Australia, abuse is a normal part of their life, and for a senator to talk as though abuse is somehow acceptable is disgusting.

As the days went on and the public condemnation of Leyonhjelm grew, his excuses and story changed, but the insults to and innuendo about me continued. My lawyers had written him a letter, asking him to stop repeating his sexist and defamatory remarks, but he refused to do so.

Then Prime Minister Malcolm Turnbull, sports heroes, church leaders and commentators called on the senator to stop what he was doing and apologise, but he was never going to. For him, this was a big game. He didn't care who he offended or who he hurt. He didn't care that the message he was sending to young girls and boys across the country was that disrespect and harassment of women were okay. Suddenly, he had more media attention than ever before, and he was lapping it up. An accidental senator whom no one had heard of was suddenly a person of interest, and he was doing it all off the back of attacking my character and personal reputation. He was rude, obnoxious and unremorseful.

In the midst of the media storm, I oscillated between wanting to hide and knowing I had to fight back. Not just for me, but for women and girls everywhere who were watching on in horror. No woman deserves to be harassed in her workplace, and no girl deserves to grow up thinking that being bullied for being a woman is okay.

Slut-shaming is a thing. It happens to women everywhere, and it was happening to me. I was lucky to be in the privileged position of being able to do something about it. I could hit back.

Then my daughter came home from school one day and told me kids were talking in the classroom about what Leyonhjelm had been saying. One boy told her, 'I saw on the news that your mum has lots of boyfriends.'

'That's a lie,' she said, standing up for herself, and for me.

'David Leyonhjelm is suggesting, because he can't win an argument … that I am sexually promiscuous,' I told ABC Radio. 'He's slut-shaming me.

'Women right around this country know it. Men, decent men, know it. And I'm not prepared to sit here and be intimidated and bullied. It's offensive, it's inflammatory and he has shown over and over again that he's unfit to be in parliament.'

My office was inundated with supportive letters, phone calls and messages from both men and women across the country, outraged at how I had been treated. Hundreds of letters detailed stories of other women who had been bullied and intimidated at work, or school, or at sports clubs, through rumour, sexual slurs and innuendo. 'Thank you for saying what so many of us are too afraid to say,' one woman wrote. 'For years I've been subjected to bullying and taunts like this at my work, and until now I didn't have the courage to do anything about it. Today, I did.'

Women shared detailed accounts of having been abused or bullied. There were examples of rumours of sexual partners or behaviour being used to undermine their credibility at work, intimidate them from speaking up in meetings, or that had ruined their ability to claim the credit they were due when landing a promotion or a job.

Men contacted me, wanting to make sure I knew that there were plenty of decent blokes out there who had my back. One gentleman wrote, 'For what it's worth, as an oldish bloke I am one hundred percent supportive of you and your stand on Leyonhjelm's behaviour. Neither you nor any woman deserves such disgraceful slurs. Well done for calling him out. It's dreadful that women have to put up with this sort of crap from anyone, let alone from an elected representative in our parliament.'

Another wrote, 'Take care of yourself, and know that there are men out there who know that yes, we have to change, and we know that the women we care for should be treated better.'

It was clear from such comments that these people weren't surprised by the attitude and behaviour I had been subjected to but that they were disgusted it was occurring in the nation's parliament. With politicians and political parties so pungently on the nose, the idea that a member of parliament could behave like such a vile bully and get away with it really irked them. 'It would be bad enough had those comments and abuse come from a bogan moron in a pub. The fact that they came from a member of the Australian Parliament shames us all,' one woman exclaimed.

There were, of course, some people who thought I was overreacting. They said I was being too 'precious' about what had happened or just 'using it for my own publicity'. Leyonhjelm's supporters were in overdrive on online forums and social media, writing foul and vulgar comments: 'Sarah's always been a slut', 'Why would anyone fuck that fat arsed slut anyway?', 'She's so fat, she'd be lucky to get one of those filthy refugees she wants to bring into the country to sleep with her.' 'Face it, you are a slut. No one is trying to shame you because sluts like you have no shame.' 'Slut', 'cunt' and 'fat' regularly appeared in my Twitter mentions.

So, you get the picture. Gross, sexist and highly abusive. One man called my office and said that if I didn't stop demanding an apology from Leyonhjelm, he and his mates would come and rape me. Another threatened to rape my daughter. All these threats were reported to the Federal Police.

This abuse, and the continued harassment in the media and online from Senator Leyonhjelm, only strengthened my resolve. This wasn't about me anymore, this was about the girls in schools across the country who needed to know they have a right to be treated with respect, and a right to express an opinion without fear of being shut down and bullied. Young women need to see that harassment in the workplace is not acceptable, and that if it happens to them, they should stand up and call it out. One young woman's email, in particular, reminded me that I was fighting this battle for her and the younger generation.

Hi Sarah,

I'm not sure whether you'll read this but here goes anyway.

I'm 17, female, from Hobart Tasmania, in grade 11 and I am sick of men degrading women. One week ago, my boss (an older man) called me and two other young girls in the workplace 'bitches', to our faces, twice in the space of a few minutes, for absolutely no reason at all other than to refer to us. I was taken aback and luckily it was at the end of our shift, so I left as quickly as possible. It made me feel uncomfortable and embarrassed.

I spoke to a few people I trusted about the comments he made, and I was told 'he's just an old man that doesn't know any better' and 'you'll have to put up with this for a long time yet,' and 'pick your battles.'

So I dismissed the whole incident. I dismissed being called a bitch by my own boss.

This morning I listened to the news, and heard about what David Leyonhjelm said.

Then I heard you speaking up for us, for all the women who get slut shamed, abused and degraded, for all the women who don't have the platform to speak out. You have made me think twice about the comments my boss made, and I don't think I should dismiss his behaviour any more.

I believe this is where it starts, dismissing one seemingly 'flippant' comment because it's not worth the hassle and soon women all over the world are dismissing a society that degrades women. I am so over accepting unacceptable behaviour. So thank you for standing up for us. Thank you for helping me understand that this is not okay. That it's not okay to feel uncomfortable and embarrassed and that I can make a stand.

> I don't know where to go from here, I am scared of speaking out, but I know enough is enough, because this is where it starts and this is where I want it to end.
>
> Thank you.

Leyonhjelm's refusal to acknowledge his bad behaviour made my decision to take legal action all the easier, as did knowing that, despite the hate and nastiness coming from his supporters, the majority of Australians felt very differently from the way he did. They want a kinder, better, more respectful society for women and girls, and they want our parliament to step up and lead the way. Former prime minister Malcolm Turnbull was right when he said that while disrespecting women doesn't always result in violence against women, all violence against women begins with disrespecting women.

'We need to have respectful workplaces where we treat each other with respect,' he said. 'Where we disagree, we disagree with respectful language, and that is why, as far as Senator Leyonhjelm is concerned, he should not have made those remarks. They were offensive, he should have withdrawn them, he should have apologised for them. It is not too late to do so.'

Along with the prime minister, the Senate expressed its collective disapproval, passing a censure motion that condemned Senator Leyonhjelm for his behaviour. It was only the fourth sanction of that magnitude to pass the Senate in a decade, and the only one moved against a senator, not a government minister.

It was an acknowledgment that as parliamentarians, we must uphold a higher standard and we need to do better than we currently are. The voters expect it, and the women and girls of Australia deserve it.

Snowflakes

There is something very wrong with the Australian media industry today. The gendered, sexualised and bullying way in which many powerful voices talk about women, and especially women in positions of authority, is getting worse. Former prime minister Julia Gillard, former president of the Australian Human Rights Commission Gillian Triggs and writer Yassmin Abdel-Magied could all attest to that.

Clearly, something has to change, but the first step in improving the tone of our national political debate is admitting that we have a problem.

There are many people out there for whom that is already too much to ask. For the rest of us, it is just the beginning.

When I first walked into the parliament in 2008, I knew that I already had three significant targets painted on my back. I was young, progressive and a woman. I was still up for the challenge, because I wanted to debate policy boldly, give as good as I got, and stick up for those who didn't have a voice in the parliament.

I knew it would be tough and I knew I'd have to be strong. What I didn't know was that, due to my age and my gender, I would have to brace myself against abusive ridicule of my private life, constant public body shaming, and an immediate campaign of sexualised rumours whipping through the parliament and the press gallery.

The continual humiliation, innuendo and insults coming from the mostly male voices in the conservative media nearly had their desired effect. There were times, in those first years, when I wanted to pack it all in and let the bastards win.

There were even times when they nearly convinced me that they were right and I wasn't worthy of the position I'd fought so hard to be in.

Even now, as a 36-year-old federal senator with more than a decade's experience in the parliament, there are still members of the media who would rather hurl insults at me than refer to me by my correct title. Paul Murray of Sky News, strangely, refers to me as 'The Hyphen', due to my double-barrelled surname, a name he took straight from the trolls on

Twitter. Others simply call me a 'silly girl' or, the Trump-devotee favourite, a 'nasty woman'.

Rather sickeningly, Michael Smith at radio station 2UE once referred to me as the 'small but perfectly formed Sarah Hanson-Young' before playing a 'skit' featuring an actor who was supposed to be me, loudly orgasming.

There is a particularly dark and angry section of our national media that needs to be called out and held to account. Sky News, *The Australian* newspaper and the News Corp tabloids, all of which are owned by Rupert Murdoch, as well as the shock jocks on the Fairfax-owned 2GB and 2UE radio stations, are regularly the worst offenders when it comes to attacking and belittling women in public life who they don't agree with. There are, it must be said, others who work within those organisations who are fine, talented and fair journalists. But I'm talking about a very specific type of political and social commentator here. They wield enormous power in shaping our national discourse, and they almost exclusively represent an ageing, angry and overwhelmingly male audience.

Many men in the Murdoch campaign machine have made a name for themselves by attacking me. Over the years, *Daily Telegraph* columnist and blogger Tim Blair alone has written dozens of articles and opinion pieces about all aspects of me and my work. Throughout these, he has referred to me, or highlighted other's references to me, as 'Sarah Hanson-Dumb', the 'Swamp Sow' and a 'cry-girl'. He has insinuated that in the future I would be transgender, have no fixed sexual identity and would be too fat to walk down the aisle of a train. He has also published a photograph of me taken shortly after I finished doing a press conference in Parliament House that he believes shows a sound engineer checking me out from behind. 'Judging by the audio guy's appreciative view,' he sniggered, 'Australia has found a local Kardashian'.

Until now, guys like Michael Smith and Tim Blair have been able to make in full public view these sleazy, gendered comments about me and specific parts of my physical appearance. They have such a strong sense of entitlement that they feel they can publish their thoughts about my arse or my 'small but perfectly formed' body, and no one will bat an eyelid. That alone tells us a lot about the sorry state of our national discourse.

Another man in the media who has an abiding fascination with me and everything I do is Ray Hadley, a shock jock from radio station 2GB. In one four-minute segment, he called me 'a dingbat', 'as mad as a meat axe', 'as silly as a cut snake', 'a dolt', 'a silly, silly woman' and, for some reason, said that I wear 'a cannabis frock with no stockings on'. His all-too-regular tirades are broadcast nationwide and come as no surprise to anyone anymore. That's because Hadley and his mates drone on and on like that, from their bully pulpits—'stupid girl' this, 'silly woman' that—in an attempt to ridicule and whip up public hatred against me, day in and day out.

Hadley regularly invites the home affairs minister, Peter Dutton, on his program, so that they can have a good old-fashioned blokey chat about how much of a silly little girl I am. They play sexist songs about me and guffaw like schoolboys, slapping each other on the back as they make disparaging comments. It's unbecoming for the two of them, especially for the federal minister involved in this, but the listeners love it, so the show goes on and on and on.

There are countless more examples of things of this nature: such as the time a national lads' magazine photoshopped my head onto a bikini model's body to try to bully me into posing semi-naked for them. I don't mention these insults to elicit sympathy. Instead, I raise them to illustrate a broader social problem, of which these examples are just a symptom. The reality is that this is the sort of treatment you can expect if you're an outspoken woman at the intersection of Australian media and politics in 2018—and it's a bloody shame.

These broadcasters and columnists to which I've been referring do, from time to time, attack men as well. They then use that fact to attempt somehow to prove that they aren't sexist. The undeniable truth, though, is that they save their most personal, vicious and hateful treatment for women. Sometimes it's Julia Gillard and sometimes it's Yassmin Abdel-Magied. Sometimes it's Gillian Triggs and sometimes it's me. Always, though, it's a woman.

And it's this specific, maniacal hatred they reserve for women that reveals these blokes as the sexists they are.

Slut

From Cleopatra to Mary Magdalene, Hester Prynne to Rachel Jackson, and Anne Boleyn to Monica Lewinsky, history and fiction are replete with women shamed, brought down and diminished because of a phenomenon we've only recently started to name, but with which women have been grappling for millennia: Slut-shaming.

Many women know what it is like to have nasty rumours and sexist gossip used against them, inside and outside of politics, but very few have been prepared to call it what it is.

This is partly because the word itself is confronting and is routinely written off as resulting from feminist hysteria. Even within feminist discourse and among feminist activists it is a loaded phrase with complicated and contested meanings.

In its simplest form, it is the shaming of someone due to their sexual behaviour—real, imagined or made up. Whether it's done via rumours, slurs or innuendo, and whether it's whispered or shouted, the effect is the same. This kind of shaming is almost exclusively reserved for women and, like most forms of sexism, is about power and control. It keeps women in rigid behavioural controls, and can be deployed to bring us down for reasons that have nothing to do with sex.

The real reason, though, that women struggle to name what is happening to them is not because we don't know what to call it but because the great power of slut-shaming as a weapon is that it is intrinsically self-concealing. We don't name it, because naming it makes the 'slut' part true in many people's minds. This works both to bully and intimidate women to stop them from stepping out of line and to silence powerfully any complaint about its use. Slut-shaming works because admitting you are being smeared with sexual innuendo can be the greatest shame of all. And the consequence of speaking out is the spreading of more innuendo.

In my own experience, male colleagues have used it as a weapon to play with my head, put me off my game and shut me up. Other times, it's been deployed to ridicule me in front of my peers, undermining my credibility while I do my job. One day, a government senator, well known for his sexist remarks, yelled out in the middle of question time, 'There goes the Green Kardashian.' as I walked over to greet members of the Afghan embassy who were visiting the parliament. Kim Kardashian has been routinely slut-shamed, so much so that her name is now synonymous with the insult. There I was, paying my regards to our visitors and a fellow senator had effectively called me a cheap slut as I was shaking their hands. I felt humiliated.

Despite our reluctance to name it, slut-shaming happens so much that it is normalised to the point where, often, only the victim knows it has occurred. Others around them are seemingly unaware of the crippling effect of such comments, rumours and taunts on the woman's confidence and ability to keep going, her head held high, pretending nothing has happened.

Women know that to acknowledge they have been victims of sexual slurs and rumour is to bear the brunt of them. The consequence of speaking out is more shame and the spreading of more innuendo. It is a horrible dilemma. Divorced women and single mothers are particularly vulnerable to slut-shaming. Without a male 'protector' as a barrier, it is easy for rumours of promiscuity to be made up, spread and believed. Single mothers have often been characterised in fiction as 'loose' women, dangerous to 'wandering' men, *The Scarlet Letter* being a case in point.

Feminists have spent decades pushing the boundaries of socially 'acceptable' behaviour for women. One of the biggest dividends of their efforts has been our increasing autonomy over our own bodies. It would be easy to understand slut-shaming as a response to this newfound freedom but, in reality, our greater sense of freedom gave us the ability to begin to share our experiences with one another; to realise these kinds of attacks weren't right, they weren't rare and they weren't one-off experiences. That has been the real power of the feminist movement—allowing women to talk to one another about their experiences and then organise to change what happens to them.

Before my critics accuse me of being a 'feminazi' or a wowser, let me be the first to say that slut-shaming and harassment are not the same as flirting with or showing a person affection. It is designed to hurt or punish, while flirting, on the other hand, is fun.

There's a Coalition senator who calls me 'babe', and 'Ser-bear', a name friends at high school called me that was, and is, endearing. It's friendly, it's affectionate, and his use of it has never been demeaning or predatory. Mature adults know the difference between being friendly and flirting, and the difference between flirting and sexist put-downs. This isn't actually hard; it's called civility. Women can instantly tell the difference between a sleaze and a gentlemen. Decent men can too.

In the case of Cleopatra, and other historic figures, their power, intellect and political cunning are diminished as their legacies are reduced to speculation about their sexual relationships. Diminishing these legacies adds to the normalisation of men being the only real leaders and erases women's history. In the case of Mary Magdalene and Monica Lewinsky, we see clearly the different standards applied to men and women, where, for one gender, sexual relationships are viewed as heroic conquests or, at least, titillating, excusable foibles; and, for the other, they can be life destroying.

The power of slut-shaming has long been its ability to hide in plain sight while demanding the silence of its victims. When something doesn't have a name, it's very hard to talk about and to resist.

Calling out slut-shaming is still a momentous and perilous task, and not everyone who has experienced its chilling effect is able to speak up. Those of us in the privileged position to do so can and should. Naming it breaks the silence it creates and calling it out breaks its power.

Nursery rhymes

The last week of parliament at the end of the year is always chaotic. There's a mad rush by the government to get legislation passed before everyone heads off on their summer holidays, with festive functions and last-minute negotiations frantically squeezed into the late-night sittings.

The last day is renowned for running into the early hours of the next morning, with debates over amendments. In one of these late-night sessions, in 2014, I was on my feet, debating a bill I had fought for months to stop. It was the Abbott government's policy of

Temporary Protection Visas. It was designed to stop anyone getting permanent protection, residency or citizenship if they had arrived in Australia by boat, even if they were found to be legitimate refugees. Essentially, it was creating a lifetime of limbo for thousands of asylum-seeker families.

The debate had been going for hours, the government not having secured the numbers from the Senate crossbench until well into the evening. I was trying to amend the bill to put some safeguards and review mechanisms in place to stop refugee children, in particular, being classed as 'illegals' for the rest of their lives. Most senators weren't participating in the debate, so would come and go from the chamber only when the bells would ring for a vote. Being the last night of the year, there were several Christmas parties and functions on in the building.

I had been in the chamber all night. As I was on my feet, arguing my points, a fellow senator walked into the chamber and started interjecting. He was yelling various things, none of them related to the amendment being debated. 'No one likes you, Sarah,' he sniggered at me from a nearby chair. He was being rude and obnoxious, trying to throw me off my game. I called on the chair to intervene and the senator was called to order. 'Senator Bernardi, you are not in your place. You should not be interjecting in any case, but it is even more disorderly to be doing it from where you are.'

I later discovered the Liberals were hosting drinks for their party members in the lounge right next to the chamber.

Over the next hour, despite being asked to stop, Senator Bernardi continued to walk in and out of the chamber, often just to heckle me. He would repeatedly distract me, and then walk out when the chair called him to order. It became increasingly apparent that he was enjoying himself.

He kept moving around the chamber, getting closer and closer to my seat, until he was sitting on the bench next to mine. As I stood, arguing my position on the current clause of the legislation, Senator Bernadi, who was still a member of the Liberal Party at the time, started singing nursery rhymes in my ear. He was leaning in, close to me, singing his songs, almost in a whisper.

He then said the name of a man he insinuated I had slept with.

Again, he did all of this while I was on my feet, speaking. It was creepy and I wasn't sure what to do. I didn't want to draw attention to it because that seemed even more embarrassing, and the last thing I wanted was to bring more focus to the rumours he was spreading. I tried hard to pretend I wasn't listening. I kept speaking to the almost empty chamber about the very serious legislation we were supposed to be debating. He got louder, wanting me to react and, finally, I did.

'Sometimes I wonder whether we should have breathalysers at the doors in this place,' I said to the chair.

'Senator Hanson-Young, resume your seat. There is no requirement for that. Senator Bernardi, I would ask you to remain quiet—silent, in fact.' I continued my speech about the amendment but the Hansard record shows that Senator Bernardi went on to interrupt me several more times before the night ended, taking no heed of the chair's warning.

Sometime past midnight, the government's legislation passed, without the amendment. I went home, exhausted and saddened that I couldn't stop what I knew was a bad policy. But I was also upset at myself. I knew I should have called out what had happened in the chamber, but instead I had stayed silent. It was because I didn't want to show weakness. I didn't want to be shamed.

For weeks after that, what had happened played on my mind. Should I have insisted Senator Bernardi be thrown out? Why was his obnoxious behaviour my fault? What was I afraid of? Anyone watching in the chamber that night must have seen what he was doing, but no one leapt to my defence. Why? Did they, like me, think that by ignoring him, he'd eventually grow bored and give up? Do bullies ever really grow bored, or are they always having too much fun bullying for that?

Little did I know, I wasn't the only one who had been thinking about what had happened. A week before parliament was to resume, in February, then senator Glenn Lazarus called for a zero-alcohol policy and breath testing of all politicians before they were allowed to vote on legislation. In an interview with ABC Radio in Brisbane, Senator Lazarus told listeners that he had witnessed me being 'abused' in the Senate after a late-night sitting where fellow senators had been drinking. Senator Lazarus left the Senate in July 2016, three years earlier than expected, after losing his seat to Pauline Hanson in Malcolm Turnbull's disastrous double-dissolution election.

In August 2018 Pauline Hanson voted against the Senate's censure of Senator Leyonhjelm over his sexist behaviour towards me. She supported his disgraceful comments and voted to protect him, but, in the end, the censure passed, by just one vote.

I wonder what Glenn Lazarus would have done if he was still there. My gut says he would have voted for decency, and respect, both for his female colleagues and for the parliament itself.

Oldest trick in the book

Sexist slurs and rumours have been used to undermine women in the parliament for as long as women have been there. Long before women were even allowed to be elected and sit in the parliament, some were said to have only got their job in a male politician's office because they were either having sex with him or he fancied having sex with her. Today, female journalists up in the press gallery still battle the rumour mill that serves to undermine them and their craft. Women journalists tell me about the frustration of knowing that delivering a news scoop will often be followed by whispers that the only way they got the story was because they 'must have' flirted with the particular minister.

For Labor MP Emma Husar, what started as a complaint from a disgruntled former staffer over how she ran her office quickly turned into a smutty public campaign to discredit her. I don't pretend to know all the ins and outs of what happened, but what is clear and on the public record paints a disturbing picture of a successful, smart woman brought down by smut and smears.

The role the media played in this campaign was lethal. What had previously been rumour and innuendo in the halls and offices of parliament, used internally to intimidate her, was soon used to slaughter her public reputation.

The member for Lindsay was accused of poor staff management, with complaints about the types of tasks her staff had been asked to do. She also brought her autistic son's dog into the office at times. The New South Wales Labor Party was investigating the complaints and a review had been commissioned. Newspapers and other media outlets had been tipped off that an investigation was underway, but that wasn't enough to really tarnish her political reputation. So, beyond staff-management issues and questions of her use of parliamentary entitlements, claims of sexualised behaviour, and even of staff members bearing witness to their boss 'flirting', were leaked to the press. The most lewd of all the allegations was that this single mother of three kids had exposed herself, *Basic Instinct* style, to a fellow MP while in his office. Both Husar and the named MP,

Jason Clare, refuted the claims immediately, but they were still published. And, as with all hot media stories and clickbait, the refuted claims were republished, and republished, and republished, by media outlets across the country. The damage was done.

Those of us in political circles knew instantly that the first-term MP from Sydney could not come back from this. There were too many lingering questions about where the line of truth was. The insinuation was clear—if she couldn't manage to keep her underpants on or legs closed, how would she be any good at managing her office? The clear insinuation was she was not fit to be an MP. 'It doesn't matter that it's not true, she can't survive this,' one seasoned Canberra MP said, summing up how so many people saw it.

It wasn't just political opponents from the other side of the chamber saying these things; the chatter in the Labor Party was unstoppable. Labor heavyweights, inside and outside the parliament, made it clear she would have to step aside. The Labor people I spoke to at the time just shook their heads, knowing how unfair but inevitable it all was. As they were more worried about shutting down the negative press than protecting one of their own from public humiliation, murmurs of a preselection challenge started to spread. It was clear Husar would not be able to stay on the team beyond the next election. While the public commentary was that 'She needs to do what's right for her and her family', the internal message was clear: 'She needed to do the right thing by the party', which was to fall on her sword.

A week later, the report of the internal investigation was handed down. It found there was no reason for the MP to resign, and that there was little basis for the complaints. But Husar, who had endured weeks of public shaming due to the deliberate leaking of lewd sexualised rumours, had already announced she was quitting politics.

Was Emma Husar slut-shamed? Yes, she was. Brutally, publicly, and with the ultimate price being her political career.

Husar's treatment both by parts of the media and individuals within her own party has been disgusting, and was nothing more than sexualised insults designed to destroy her credibility in the age-old way. Tragically, in her case, it worked. Her short time as a young, female politician is over, before she had even got a chance to recontest the election. Her career destroyed. And all for what? Because a man who didn't get along with his female boss thought spreading rumours about her going sans underwear was fair? Or because she dared to tell a bloke who worked in her office he wasn't up to the job? She upset the sense of entitlement of the Labor boys' club and was punished, in full sight.

When I first heard Emma Husar had described what happened to her as 'slut-shaming', I felt a sense of relief: *Thank god someone else feels empowered to say it*. It felt like proof that calling out this nastiness does work in breaking the silence. Naming it for what it is does help other women stand up and speak out. But, actually, I'm angry. We should all be angry. A strong woman, who managed to juggle being a politician (and in a marginal seat!) and a single mum at the same time has been forced out of politics; another woman gone, chewed up and spat out. A woman who has dedicated her public life to victims of domestic violence and to support for children with disabilities has been brought down by a sexist attack on her character and by false claims about her reputation.

To those of us watching, what happened to Emma Husar was another clinical case of a woman in the public eye being set up, ripped down and hung out to dry. These nasty rumours should never have cost her being a member of parliament. If she'd been a bloke, she would still be an MP after the next election. Heavens, Barnaby Joyce, who slept with one of his staff, fathered a child from the affair, and admitted in a tell-all book to chasing women and being drunk on the job, has just been welcomed back to a plum appointment the prime minister has created for him. The member for Lindsay did none of those things, yet she is the one forced out of politics.

Women of all stripes

As a woman, the higher you get in the once exclusively male world of politics, the more your existence is considered an unwelcome intrusion and the more ferociously your opponents try to tear you down.

Never has this been more clearly shown than when Julia Gillard became the first female prime minister of Australia.

First, I think it's important to reflect on the fact that it took more than a hundred years and twenty-six male prime ministers before we had a woman in the top job. That alone reveals how, when it comes to selecting people for positions of power in this country, merit is not the sole consideration. In fact, when looking at some of the people who occupy the government benches in parliament right now, you may be forgiven for thinking that merit is barely a factor at all.

When women, who are slightly more than 50 per cent of the population, have made up less than 4 per cent of Australian prime ministers, there is something seriously wrong. Either men are somehow intrinsically better at running the country, or fundamentally sexist power structures actively discriminate against women making it to high office. I know which one of those two I'd put my money on.

I also want to recognise that, in Gillard's time as prime minister, she achieved many significant reforms for Australia. These include the Royal Commission into Institutional

Responses to Child Sexual Abuse, the National Disability Insurance Scheme, and working with the Greens to put in place a world-leading scheme to tackle global warming. Securing these outcomes was made all the more impressive by the fact that she did it while weathering a vicious, gender-based campaign of ridicule and smears from the national media.

Gillard was a prime minister for whom around half of the country's media showed pure and open contempt. They argued policy, for sure, but too often she was criticised for what she wore, how she looked and how she talked. In addition to that, prominent radio personalities joked about the method in which she should be killed, and shameful remarks were made about her being to blame for the fact that her father died while she was in office. While in politics criticism comes with the job, this hysterical level of scorn and personal attack was peculiar to her, the first and only woman to lead the country. That, of course, was no coincidence.

One of the images that will forever define this aspect of Julia Gillard's treatment as prime minister came when Tony Abbott stood in front of signs with 'DITCH THE WITCH' and 'JULIAR…. BOB BROWNS BITCH' plastered across them. The signs were outrageous, not only because they were so inflammatory, but because they betrayed the real reason so many people hated her—finally, someone had said it. She was a woman and that meant she was a witch; also, that she was nothing more than a bitch who was being played by the real men of politics.

I will always be thankful for, and proud of, Bob Brown's response to these hateful insults to Gillard. He was one of the few political voices who offered support to her at that time. He recognised that the national conversation in relation to her and her leadership was no longer rational.

'I just think the degree of relentless criticism of this prime minister coming from male commentators, it's probably all subconscious, but is sexist and quite ridiculous at times,' Bob Brown said, adding, 'People are incredibly impressed with her ability to deal with what is chucked at her, and so am I.'

I hope that the then prime minister heard those words in the spirit they were intended: as a gesture of peace and goodwill across the political aisle that too often divides us.

There were also times when Gillard was criticised for not being feminine enough, like in 2005, when a photoshoot in her home's kitchen revealed the apparently unspeakable sin of having a nearly empty fruit bowl. In response, people accused her of neglecting her feminine household duties and some said it was a telling reflection of her life decision to be 'intentionally barren'. The comments were both unnecessarily personal and completely unguarded in their sexism.

Other times, she was criticised for going too far the other way and being too feminine. There was the *Australian Women's Weekly* cover shoot that showed her knitting a toy kangaroo for Wills' and Kate's royal baby. The photo caused an eruption of outrage across the country. Many people said that she was playing the gender card by portraying herself in a feminine light, while Andrew Bolt, from Rupert Murdoch's News Corp, ridiculed the prime minister for indulging in a hobby 'now synonymous with mad old aunts'.

After years of Gillard being told that she had to show her softer side, it came as no surprise to many of us that, when she did, she was instantly slammed for it.

Like so many women in this country, she simply couldn't win, because the system set her up to fail. As a woman in public life, if you're soft, it means you're weak; and if you're tough, it means you're a bitch. There's practically no safe space to occupy between those two alternatives, and if you stray too far one way or the other, the reprisals are swift, fierce and often severe enough to end a career.

I hold conflicting opinions about Gillard's time as prime minister. Being Australia's first female leader was a momentous achievement that helped to move our nation towards gender equality. The fact that she reached the office of prime minister means that young girls across the country now know the same is possible for them. That alone is an extraordinary thing to do for Australian women, and she did it at significant cost to herself, her privacy and her family life.

At the same time, I wish she had used her position to do so much more for women in a practical, real-world way.

This conflict between appreciation of and frustration with Gillard was on full display during her famous misogyny speech. It was a brilliant example of her at her best. She took on the haters and tore them apart. Through that one inspired act, she made it easier for women, including me, to call out sexism publicly in the future when we saw it.

Julia Gillard's speech was a watershed moment for women but what's been largely lost in the fog of memory is that, on the very same day, her government savagely cut the level of funding for single parents, almost all of whom are single mothers. The fact that this was done on the same day she delivered that seminal speech left many of us confused as to what Gillard really stood for. History will be much kinder to Gillard than the political class at the time.

One thing we can all agree on, though, is that women have it tough in politics, regardless of which political party they belong to.

Julie Bishop knows all too well about the difficulties of being a woman in conservative circles. Despite being the most popular, experienced and electable leadership candidate in the recent coup that ended Malcolm Turnbull's time as prime minister, Bishop was summarily snubbed by her colleagues. They opted, instead, for a contest between two men who are extremely unpopular with voters. It seemed the only thing the warring factions of the Liberal Party could agree on was that it's better to lose an election than have a woman in charge.

Sexism doesn't explain everything about why the then foreign affairs minister was overlooked for the top job, but it goes a long way.

Julie Bishop summed up the pathetic display when a reporter asked her if the Liberal

Party will ever be able to bring itself to support a popular female leader. 'When we find one, I'm sure we will,' she responded with a pointedly raised eyebrow.

And that's one of the major problems with the way women are treated in Australian politics today. Many are forced to leave before reaching their full potential because of the toxic nature of the work environment or the fact that their careers stall once reaching a certain level.

When Liberal MP Julia Banks revealed that she had been bullied and intimidated by members of her own party and, as a result, would be resigning, I was impressed by her courage. As another woman who has experienced years of bullying in the parliament, I wanted to reach out and support her, and I didn't care that she was from a rival political party.

There are many people in Canberra who think that party loyalty should come before all else. To them, any suffering by a person from another party is a good thing, and any failure of another party to protect its female MPs from bullying is to be privately celebrated and then publicly exploited for maximum political benefit.

I decided some time ago, however, that creating an environment where people can work together to improve the culture for women in parliament, regardless of their party affiliation, is more important to me than scoring political points at every opportunity.

I wasn't surprised when others saw revelations of bullying from women within the Liberal Party as nothing more than an opportunity to criticise the conservatives. Even some within the Greens thought we should sink the boot in, rather than support the women who were speaking out. It just showed me once again that politics, in general, has a problem with women, and that it's not confined to any one party or side.

In saying this, I must be honest—I should have spoken up more when Peta Credlin, chief of staff to former prime minister Tony Abbott, was subject to her own onslaught of smear and innuendo. Peta copped it on two fronts. She was a strong, powerful woman but also in the position of being a member of staff, who aren't allowed their own microphone, which meant the silencing effect was doubly stifling. Women like me, who know what it feels like to be reduced to these rumours and smut, should have done more. Yes, she is a political opponent on most issues but, as Madeleine Albright puts it so neatly, there's a special place in hell for women who hide behind excuses like this.

Emma Husar, Julie Bishop, Julia Banks and Peta Credlin have all been let down by the Australian political system in different ways. None of these woman are perfect, of course, but only the wilfully ignorant could miss how significant their gender was when it came to how they were treated. The same, of course, is true for Julia Gillard.

The toxic boys' club of Australian politics has become more combative towards women and increasingly tribal over the years. As the level of hyper-partisanship has grown, bullying and intimidation have been all but normalised and women continue to cop the brunt of it.

It doesn't matter what side of the chamber we come from because this isn't about party politics anymore. It's about decency and respect, not just to each other as MPs but respect for the people who elected us. No woman, or man, deserves to show up to work and be harassed, bullied or intimidated. It's not okay in the workplace, it's not okay in our homes and our parliament should set a better example.

It's always disappointing to see a woman quit in the face of a culture that so many of us know needs to change. The first step in fixing the environment, though, is to break the silence. Women and decent men must call out unacceptable behaviour whenever and wherever they see it, whether that's in the chamber or within their own party rooms.

The next step is for all sides of politics to welcome, promote and elect more women in their ranks. When there are more women around the chamber, cultural change will happen. After ten years in this place, I know firsthand that the people who elected us to represent them are better served when there are more, not fewer, women in parliament.

Child's play

Anyone who's watched parliament question time knows that it is often little more than a public display of brawling politicians, sprinkled with some non-answers from ministers and the odd 'zinger' from the Opposition. In the midst of all the carry-on, I often find myself looking up to see the visiting school children watching us from the public gallery. It's hard not to feel a sense of embarrassment; kind of like when you drop a swear word at home and your 11-year-old daughter pulls you up briskly. It is a reminder that as adults, it is so often a case of practising 'Do as I say, not as I do.'

I've often pondered that if our nation's children had the opportunity to speak during question time, how the tone of the place would change. It would certainly be more respectful, less aggressive, and some answers may even be given. I would guess too, that the issues raised would be focused on the future of the country, not just the latest Newspoll or the week's biggest gotcha moment. But, if nothing else, more children in parliament would certainly lower the amount of verbal abuse hurled across the floor of the chamber. Politicians would be on their best behaviour, in fear of being scolded by a representative of the next generation.

In 2017, I was thrilled when my Greens colleague Senator Larissa Waters became the first woman to breastfeed her baby in the federal parliament. It made headlines, and for all the right reasons. It was a celebration that finally our parliament had caught up with the modern world's expectations that working women need not be excluded from their duties as leaders simply because they are new mothers. Changes were being made over in the House of Representatives, too. Female MPs were finally allowed to breastfeed in the chamber, and could be absent during a vote, without penalty, if their child required care. These arrangements have given more access and equality to women on all sides of politics, so that they can get on with both public service and motherhood.

Like all progressive reforms, these changes didn't happen by themselves. They were fought for across party lines by a group of younger MPs who decided it was time to modernise the way women, and children, were valued in the parliament. The Liberal Party's Kelly O'Dwyer and Labor's Kate Ellis and Amanda Rushworth all worked hard to make sure they and their electorates would no longer be disenfranchised simply because they were now mums with bubs in tow.

When it comes to role models, it would be remiss not to acknowledge New Zealand prime minister Jacinda Ardern: a young, female leader with a strong progressive agenda, positive attitude, and a baby born on the job. Despite her modest insistence that this is nothing remarkable, the power of examples like this are undeniable. Girls and women across the globe are clearly seeing equality in a whole new light, with leadership and motherhood not as opposing choices. The prime minister's warmth and candour with the public as she learns to juggle parenthood and politics in such a highly scrutinised environment are refreshing and powerful. Australia has come a long way in encouraging women in politics but, as is too often the case with rugby, New Zealand is still in front.

It's hard to imagine but, only nine years ago, the rules in the Senate and the attitude that accompanied them were very different.

It was a Thursday afternoon, at the end of a long sitting week, and the parliament was debating a Greens bill to ban junk food advertising during children's television shows. Kora was two years old at the time, and in Canberra, as per usual; when she was little, she always travelled with me for each parliamentary sitting week. She was about to leave for the airport, with the nanny I employed, to fly back home to South Australia without me. I had meetings scheduled on the Friday in Canberra, and Kora had her regular day at childcare in Adelaide. Despite our busy schedule and frequent travelling, I'd made a decision early on that it was important she had some regular time with other children, and not spend all of her week in my office, in meetings and around adults. Socialisation and exposure to early childhood education were important, so I always tried to ensure she would be at home on Fridays to enjoy a day at childcare. It had become a ritual of ours that, on days where I had to stay behind and she would fly home, we would take a walk along the Parliament House corridors and, if the weather permitted, enjoy some fresh air in the internal gardens, before saying goodbye.

We were just outside the back of the Senate chamber when the bells rang for the final vote on the junk food bill. When the 'bells ring' in the Senate, members have four minutes to get from wherever they are into the chamber, to take their seat and be counted for the vote. It is essentially a head count. Those voting yes sit on the government side of the chamber; those voting no sit on the Opposition's side. The nanny was packing up the last of Kora's belongings in the office and getting ready to depart for the airport. Being on my own with Kora, I knew that if I ran upstairs to my office, dropped her off and then ran back down, I would miss the vote. It's never a good look to miss a vote and, being that it was on a Greens bill, my doing so would have annoyed my colleagues immensely. In the ten years I've been in the Senate, I have only missed a vote three times, always because I was out of earshot of the bells.

We were right outside the chamber, so, without thinking much about it, I took her in with me to vote. Unlike parliamentary debates, where you have to speak from your seat, votes are relatively informal. People sit anywhere they like as long as they are on the right side for casting an 'Aye' or 'No'. The only rule is that once you have taken your seat, the Senate doors are locked and you can't move.

As we walked in and sat down, Kora was happy and content. She's always been a friendly and relaxed child, which has helped to make both of our lives easier to manage.

I've always felt lucky that I had a kid who could go with the flow, making it much less stressful if I had to have her by my side at meetings or take her to events.

We sat next to my fellow Greens senators Bob Brown, Christine Milne, Rachel Siewert and Scott Ludlam.

Bob had been leading the debate on the bill to ban junk food advertising. While parents and health experts backed the move, the big media moguls and sugar industry players were strongly opposed. They were putting profits before kids and it wasn't surprising in the slightest.

My assumption had been that after casting my vote, I would quickly run Kora to the waiting car, she would head off to the airport, and I would see her in a day or two. Little did I know what a furore these four minutes would cause.

'Lock the doors,' the Senate president, Labor senator John Hogg, ordered. The whips got up to start the count, but the president stopped. He had noticed Kora sitting quietly on my lap.

Under the Senate standing orders, anyone not a member of the chamber is determined to be a 'stranger'. The president demanded that she be removed.

Bob Brown jumped to his feet to protest the decision, but Senator Hogg was unrelenting. Holding Kora in my arms, I walked to the back of the chamber.

The noise grew as members from all sides started interjecting, some in support of Kora staying, and others opposed. Kora became aware something was wrong. And, as the Senate security officer went to take her from my arms, she started to scream. Instinctively, I resisted handing her over to the guard. She was clinging to me as if we were teetering on the edge of a cliff and there was no way I was giving her to a stranger when she was in a state like this.

Thankfully, a staffer from Senator Brown's office, who had seen the incident unfolding on the internal TV stream, had bolted to the chamber. The guards opened the door, just enough for me to pass the crying child through it. The president ordered the counting of the vote to continue. As I sat back down, the chamber that is usually insulated from external noise was unable to block out the echoing sound of my baby girl howling outside.

The vote was lost. Only the five Greens senators and an Independent voted to stop junk food advertising being aimed at children, with Labor and Liberal members voting together to sink the bill. Upset, I rushed back to my office. The phones were ringing off the hook and my daughter was sitting on the couch, my staff consoling her. Before I decided what to do next, the evening TV news bulletins broke into live crosses to Parliament House, and the media circus began.

The ensuing debate over working mums, work-life balance and the expectations of child-friendly workplaces went on for days. Shock jocks were in overdrive and conservative newspaper columnists penned their outrage. The leader of the National Party in the Senate, Barnaby Joyce, labelled the incident a 'stunt'. He said I 'used the child as a prop, and the Senate as [my] stage', suggesting that it was a premeditated event. I was hurt, angry and offended that anyone would suggest I would use my family like this to get some pithy media attention. Call me cynical, but I reckon if I'd been a father trying to juggle my family demands, the response would have been very different: positive, in fact. Joyce, who was still a Senator at the time, hadn't even been in the chamber when the event happened. He'd missed the vote, saying he was too busy doing other things. Attacking me, he said, 'There are 21 million people who rely on the way the Senate votes, you've got to take that job seriously.' So seriously, apparently, he couldn't even be bothered showing up. Pathetic.

Weeks later, Joyce approached me as we walked into the Senate for morning prayers and put his hand on my shoulder. 'No hard feelings; it's all part of the game,' he said.

'Yes, hard feelings,' I shot back, swiping his hand away. 'You're a disgrace. You know that wasn't a stunt and you said it anyway. You've accused me of being a bad mother and a bad senator.'

Joyce shrugged. 'I've got four children and I've only spent seven days at home with them this year ... I'm not complaining,' he said.

'Well, I reckon that makes you the crap parent, not me,' I said and walked into the chamber. Of course, after the recent excruciating media coverage of Barnaby Joyce's private life, it turns out I was right.

It took eight years after Kora became the youngest person to be evicted from the parliament for the Senate standing orders to be amended. But as Senator Waters sat nursing her youngest daughter, I was reminded that progress can and does happen. Attitudes can soften and change, as can their advocates.

During the right-wing media pile-on, News Limited columnist David Penberthy had disparagingly labelled me the 'pin-up girl for the work-life balance brigade', fuming in an opinion piece that I was wrong to have taken my daughter to parliament. He may very well have believed that back then; however, I suspect his view may have changed. Penberthy is now married to Labor MP Kate Ellis and, a proud dad, he announced live on breakfast radio his wife's second pregnancy.

Both their kids have accompanied their mum to Canberra in recent years, and now, due to changes that we have all fought for, they are more welcome than ever in Parliament House.

Yes, change can happen. And, I still believe, the more children we have around, the better the adults will behave.

'Nasty woman'

Plenty has been written about the increase of ultra-conservative voices, and the influence they have on public debate, in the US, UK and Europe, as well as here in Australia, whether it's the political muscle Fox News exerts in the US, the rise of UKIP in Britain, and the shock Brexit vote, or Marine Le Pen putting up a formidable, if unsuccessful, challenge in the most recent French presidential race. Of course, Donald Trump's election to the White House exemplifies more than anything else this far-right, anti-immigration, anti-environment, anti-planet agenda, which also happens to be anti-woman.

We have our own copycat commentators and politicians, who dance on the fringes, with little credibility, but find their place in feeding the outrage machine that sustains our 24/7 media cycle and social-media newsfeeds. So lazy and uninspired are these Trump-lite politicians and Fox-frenzy commentators that they simply import biased 'studies', re-hashed political debates and outrage topics straight from conservative think tanks and political voices overseas. Heavens, even the marketing materials have been ripped off, with one Australian politician creating their own 'Make Australia Great Again' hat in a desperate effort to ride the Trump wave here in Oz.

And while I am strongly optimistic that the vast majority of Australians don't share the extreme conservative views the Fox-ified parts of our media promote, it would be naive not to be wary of the impact that Americanisation is having on parts of our national conversation. From the issues that are elevated to national prominence, to the tone these debates take, there has undoubtedly been growth in the hyper-partisan and divisive nature of politics. As right-wing voices like One Nation and Pauline Hanson compete for their small share of the pie, they are locked in a race to the bottom to be as outrageous as possible, so as to bolster their base. Competing for airtime and attention means even members of the major parties participate in this race to out-Trump each other.

Over recent years, there has been a very noticeable slide to the right on immigration, race and even on the science of climate change. Who would have thought that in 2018, with all the available technology and abundance of cheap renewable energy, that the strength of one's devotion to coal would become an ideological linchpin for the right of Australian politics? The outrage machine has even turned the humble shopping bag into a symbol of division as, not long ago, right-wing commentators were in a frenzy over moves to ban single-use plastic bags in supermarkets. The plastic bag was held up as an emblem for the good old days, before political correctness took over. The right to free plastic bags was equated to the right to freedom of speech. Seriously, it was crackpot populism in overdrive.

But the media love it, so they keep going with it, no matter how crazy it gets or what the consequences may be. In an environment where bad behaviour is rewarded with news headlines and slots on breakfast TV, as well as after-dark talk shows, the more aggressive and offensive, the better. If anyone complains, they are instantly labelled 'snowflakes' or 'political-correctness Nazis'. The confected fight over freedom of speech has become a lazy, yet deliberate, excuse for 'freedom to abuse' without rhyme, reason or consequence. This all leads to an increasingly toxic culture, where political debate is more and more aggressive and bullying, and intimidation is all but normalised. This doesn't just affect women, of course, men are victims of abuse too, but in the mire of political ugliness, women always cop the worst of it.

People often say that the parliament is a place of 'rough and tumble' debate, as though that somehow excuses hostility and conflict that wouldn't be accepted in other workplaces. This, in and of itself, makes it harder for women to confront bad behaviour and bullying when they experience it, for fear of being dismissed or ridiculed as being weak and not up to the job. The barriers to women speaking up and calling out abuse in the broader community are amplified in an environment where strength and resilience are among the most valued commodities.

Yes, the parliament is robust and adversarial by its very nature. Question time is just one of the daily rituals that entrenches this fact. In the British House of Commons, from which we inherited our Westminster system, the distance across the floor between the government and opposition benches is 3.96 metres, the exact length of two swords. This is designed to remind the MPs that battles once fought with violence are now fought with words. 'This may be true,' former Victorian premier John Brumby wryly points out in his memoirs, 'but the contests are quite gladiatorial nonetheless'.

Parliament is a tough place for anyone, but, again, for women it's worse. However, as the intensity of the battles increases while hyper-partisan and extreme elements of the political spectrum compete for space, female members of parliament are starting to speak up and say, 'Enough is enough.' I believe that the public will reward those who have the courage to call out bullying and demand a better standard of behaviour, because the voters' patience with politicians behaving badly is running thin. They have figured out that if MPs are spending all their time bickering and sledging each other, there's not much attention being given to the real issues facing the nation. While education levels drop and inequality grows, while the divide between the wealthy and everyone else gets wider, and our natural environment suffers from pollution and neglect, voters look on at the wrestling match in Canberra with dismay.

It is, increasingly, female politicians who are blowing the whistle on the unsavoury culture in parliament. As we name it and call it out, we speak for the rights of voters as well as ourselves. Populist conservatives, like One

Nation and their ilk, who say they care about those who are doing it tough are frauds. Their contribution to the parliament is plain old trickery, thuggery, and a far-right agenda that benefits their self-interest and nothing more. They spend more time debating motions to cut women's access to abortion than they do arguing for a raise in the dole, which hasn't been increased for over twenty years. Rather than fighting to ensure every child gets access to a quality education—one of the best ways to lift families out of poverty—these Fox-fanned politicians are out calling for hand guns and tasers to be more readily available on the streets.

Along with policies and agendas that attack multiculturalism and weaken gun control, the 'freedom of speech' crusade is now being used to undermine gender equality, and the rights of women to live our lives freely and without intimidation and harassment.

In the past twelve months alone, there have been eight motions brought forward by conservative male senators attempting to limit women's control over our own bodies. These have ranged from reducing access to abortions and reproductive rights, to attacking programs and organisations that work to stop domestic and sexual violence against women. All of these motions, every one of them, were listed on the parliamentary notice paper for debate and voting by men. Conservative men. The debates themselves make my skin crawl.

Have these individuals no capacity for self-reflection? It seems not.

Only a few months ago, I sat in the Senate chamber while a Nationals member was trying to move a motion condemning the decriminalisation of abortions in Queensland. As he spoke, his disdain for women who were even considering terminating their pregnancies was palpable. While he ranted, a male colleague quipped that women who abort are nothing more than 'murderers'. It was a disgusting display.

Do they realise how out of touch they are? Of course not, and that is part of the problem. These are the death throes of a dwindling conservative male view that most of the country left behind years ago. Like mould in the bathroom, though, while you can scrub the tiles clean, the bits in the corner will always try to grow back if you don't keep them at bay.

Women are needed in the parliament now more than ever, to ensure that the values it represents, of a fair, inclusive and equal society, are not taken for granted or relegated to the 'job done' category. Right now, there are members of the Australian parliament who are attacking the hard-fought-for rights of women, such as our choice whether or not to become mothers. Women from all sides of politics are needed to tackle this increasing assault on our freedoms. Without female voices combating this revolting Trumpification of our politics and democracy, I shudder to think where we would end up.

For female members of the parliament, dealing with the increase in aggression and the onslaught of anti-equality rhetoric in formal debates is confronting. But what is clear is that as more women stand up and call it out, our collective courage grows. It puts the men behaving badly on notice, but, more importantly, it sends a message to the rest of the community that women and girls do have a right to be heard and respected, wherever they are.

Let's get on with it!